What Is Truth? - From Skepticism to Submission

Joshua Rhoades

Published by Joshua Paul Rhoades, 2024.

WHAT IS TRUTH? - FROM SKEPTICISM TO SUBMISSION

First edition. August 23, 2024.

ISBN: 979-8224990252

Written by Joshua Rhoades.

Also by Joshua Rhoades

Courage Under Fire: David's Stand On The Battlefield
Jonah's Journey: Voices Of Redemption And Lessons In Obedience
The Furnace Of Faith: 12 Principles From The Heat Of Faith
Whispers of Hope: Inspiring Stories of Men's Prayers In Scripture
Frontier Legends: The Oregon Dream
Elijah: A Beacon Of Boldness
HOOK, LINE & SAVIOUR - Faith Reflections from Fishing
Driven By Faith: Motor Racing Inspired Christian Life
30 Day Devotional - Bold and Strong- Coffee Devotions for a Courageous Christian Walk
Authentic Christianity: The Heart of Old Time Religion
Consider The Ant - God's Tiny Preachers
Flee Fornication: The Plea For Purity
Renewed Hope- How to Find Encouragement in God
Sounding The Call - The Voice of Conviction
The Altar - Where Heaven Meets Earth
The Bible's Battlefields- Timeless Lessons from Ancient Wars
The Sacred Art of Silence - How Silence Speaks in Scripture
Under Fire- The Sanctity of the Traditional Biblical Home
Who Is on the Lord's Side? A Call to Righteousness
What Is Truth? - From Skepticism to Submission

Introduction

In John 18:38, as Jesus stood before Pilate, bound and on trial, Pilate asked a question that has echoed through the ages: "What is truth?" It is a question that reflects not only the deep confusion and uncertainty of Pilate's moment but also a profound skepticism that pervades our world today. Pilate was not just asking a philosophical question; he was confronting the very essence of truth itself, embodied in the person of Jesus Christ. But rather than seeking an answer, Pilate dismissed the question, choosing instead the path of expediency and compromise. In doing so, he missed the profound truth standing right before him—the truth that Jesus is God incarnate, the embodiment of truth, as He declared in John 14:6: "I am the way, the truth, and the life:"

Today, society is no different. We live in an age where truth is often seen as relative, where the notion of absolute truth is dismissed as outdated or intolerant. The question "What is truth?" is as relevant now as it was two thousand years ago, as people grapple with the overwhelming barrage of information, conflicting ideologies, and moral ambiguity that define our times. Like Pilate, many today stand before the truth without recognizing it, or worse, rejecting it outright because it challenges their beliefs, their comfort, or their desires. In a world that celebrates skepticism and doubts, the truth remains steadfast, unchanging, and eternal—embodied in the person of Jesus Christ.

This book, "What Is Truth? - From Skepticism to Submission," dives into the journey that Pilate failed to complete and that society continues to resist—the journey from questioning the truth to embracing it. It challenges the prevailing notion that truth is subjective, showing that true freedom and fulfillment come not from bending truth to fit our lives, but from aligning our lives with the truth. Jesus did not merely speak the truth; He is the truth. His life, death, and resurrection are the ultimate revelations of God's truth, offering a clear and unshakable foundation in a world of shifting sands.

In this book, we explore the stark contrast between Pilate's skepticism and Jesus' unwavering declaration of truth. We examine how society today mirrors Pilate's reluctance to submit to the truth, often choosing the comfort of relativism over the challenge of living by an absolute standard. Yet, just as Pilate's refusal to embrace the truth led to tragic consequences, so too does our society face the fallout of rejecting the truth found in Jesus Christ—evident in the moral confusion, broken relationships, and deep-seated unrest that characterize our world.

But this book is not just a critique; it is a call to action, a call to move from skepticism to submission. It invites readers to confront the truth of Jesus Christ, to wrestle with the implications of His claim to be the way, the truth, and the life, and to consider what it means to submit to that truth in every aspect of life. This is not an easy journey, but it is the only path that leads to genuine peace, purpose, and freedom. As you turn these pages, you are invited to step into the truth that Pilate missed and that the world so desperately needs—to discover the transformative power of submitting to the truth that is Jesus Christ, God incarnate, the eternal and unchanging foundation of all that is real and true.

Chapter 1 – The Substance of Truth

Pilate's question, "What is truth?" speaks directly to the heart of one of the most profound and pressing issues in the human experience—the substance of truth. This question highlights the critical importance of understanding what truth truly is, especially in a world where so much seems uncertain, relative, and changeable. Truth, however, is not something that shifts with the tides of public opinion or changes based on personal perspectives. It is solid, unwavering, and absolute. The substance of truth is not subjective or dependent on individual interpretation; it is grounded in the very character of God and revealed in His Word. This means that truth is not something we can bend to fit our desires or mold to suit our circumstances. Instead, it stands firm and unchanging, like a rock that cannot be moved by the storms of life. This solid nature of truth offers us a foundation upon which we can build our lives, a reliable source of guidance in a world full of confusion and chaos. When Pilate asked, "What is truth?" he was confronting a reality that many people still struggle with today—the challenge of recognizing and accepting a truth that is greater than ourselves, one that demands humility, obedience, and reverence. This truth is not always comfortable, nor is it always easy to accept, but it is essential for living a life that is aligned with God's will and purpose. The substance of truth, as grounded in God's character, is not just a set of abstract principles or rules; it is a reflection of who God is—His holiness, His righteousness, His love, and His justice. In this way, understanding the substance of truth is intrinsically linked to understanding and knowing God Himself.

It is in His Word that this truth is most clearly revealed to us, offering us not just knowledge, but wisdom, direction, and life. The Bible, as God's Word, is the ultimate source of truth, providing a clear and authoritative standard against which all other claims of truth must be measured. This truth speaks to every aspect of our lives—our beliefs, our actions, our relationships, and our decisions. It challenges us to live in a way that reflects the reality of God's nature and His commands. It calls us to reject the falsehoods and deceptions that the world often presents as truth and to hold fast to what is true, even when it is difficult or countercultural. The substance of truth is also deeply connected to the idea of integrity and authenticity. To live according to the truth is to live with integrity, to be honest and true in all that we do, reflecting the truth of God in our own lives. This is not just about being truthful in our words, but about embodying the truth in our actions, in our character, and in our hearts. When we understand the substance of truth as being grounded in God's character, we realize that truth is not just something to be believed, but something to be lived out daily. This understanding transforms the way we approach life, giving us a clear direction and purpose, and helping us to navigate the complexities and challenges we face. It also provides us with a deep sense of security and peace, knowing that we are standing on the firm foundation of God's truth, rather than on the shifting sands of human opinion. In a world where truth is often seen as relative or negotiable, where people are encouraged to "live their truth" regardless of its alignment with reality, the substance of truth stands as a beacon of hope and clarity. It reminds us that there is a standard of truth that transcends our individual perspectives and preferences, a truth that is as solid and unchanging as the God who speaks it. Pilate's question, therefore, invites us to reflect deeply on what we believe to be true and to consider whether our understanding of truth is truly grounded in God's Word or influenced by the shifting opinions of the world. It challenges us to seek out the substance of truth with humility, recognizing that it is not something we can define for ourselves, but something that has been revealed to us by a loving and just God. As we seek to understand and embrace this truth, we are called to allow it to shape and transform every aspect of our lives, leading us into a deeper relationship with God and a more authentic expression of our faith. The substance of truth is not just a concept to be intellectually grasped; it is a living reality that must be lived out in the way we interact with others, the decisions we make, and the way we conduct our lives. It is the bedrock of our faith, the foundation upon which everything else stands, and it is as essential to our spiritual health as air is to our physical survival. In a world full of noise and conflicting messages, understanding and living according to the substance of truth is more important than ever. It is the key to navigating life with wisdom and grace, and it is the sure foundation that will sustain us through every trial and challenge we face.

Chapter 2 – The Savior as Truth

When Jesus declared, "I am the way, the truth, and the life" (John 14:6), He was revealing something profound and life-changing about Himself—that truth is not just an abstract idea, a set of rules, or a concept to be debated, but a living person, embodied in Him, the Savior of the world. In the context of John 18, where Pilate questions, "What is truth?" Jesus had already made it clear to His disciples that He is the truth. This means that truth is not something we can define on our own terms; it is not something that changes with the times or with popular opinion. Truth is found in a person, and that person is Jesus Christ. He is the embodiment of all that is true, good, and holy. To know Jesus is to know the truth, and to follow Him is to walk in the truth. This understanding transforms our relationship with truth from something cold and distant to something deeply personal and relational. When we think of truth as a person, we realize that truth is not just something to be known, but someone to be loved, trusted, and followed. Jesus, as the Savior, is the ultimate revelation of God's truth to humanity. He came to show us the way to the Father, to demonstrate through His life, death, and resurrection what it means to live in the truth. His teachings, His actions, and His very being are the standard by which all truth is measured. When He says He is the truth, He is claiming that everything about Him—His words, His character, His mission—perfectly reflects the reality of who God is and what God desires for us.

This understanding of Jesus as the truth has profound implications for our lives. It means that if we want to know what is true, we must look to Jesus. If we want to live in truth, we must follow His example. It also means that truth is not just a set of facts to be learned or doctrines to be memorized, but a relationship to be experienced. In a world where truth is often treated as relative or flexible, Jesus stands as the unchanging and eternal truth. He is the anchor that holds us steady in a sea of confusion and deception. When we anchor our lives in Jesus, we are anchoring ourselves in truth that will never fail us, never lead us astray, and never change with the whims of culture. This is why it is so important to know Jesus personally and intimately because to know Him is to know the truth that sets us free.

Moreover, Jesus as the truth is not just a comforting idea; it is a powerful reality that confronts us and calls us to change. When we encounter Jesus, we are confronted with the truth about ourselves, our sin, and our need for a Savior. His truth exposes the lies we have believed, the false identities we have clung to, and the ways we have strayed from God's perfect will. But this confrontation is not meant to condemn us; it is meant to heal us, to set us free from the bondage of sin and deception. Jesus, as the truth, offers us a new way of living, one that is rooted in God's reality rather than in the illusions of the world. His truth brings light into our darkness, clarity into our confusion, and hope into our despair.

This truth is also deeply liberating. Jesus said, "You shall know the truth, and the truth shall make you free" (John 8:32). When we embrace Jesus as the truth, we find freedom from the lies that have held us captive—lies about our worth, our purpose, and our future. We are freed from the need to prove ourselves, to earn God's love, or to live up to the impossible standards of the world. In Jesus, we find the truth of God's unconditional love, His unending grace, and His perfect plan for our lives. This truth gives us the courage to live boldly, to face challenges with confidence, and to walk in the assurance that we are loved, accepted, and secure in God's hands.

Furthermore, seeing Jesus as the truth means that we are called to a life of integrity and authenticity. If Jesus is the truth, then our lives should reflect that truth. We are called to live in a way that is consistent with who Jesus is, to be people of honesty, integrity, and faithfulness. This means rejecting the falsehoods and compromises that the world often presents and choosing instead to live according to the truth that Jesus embodies. It means being true to who God has created us to be, true to the calling He has placed on our lives, and true to the principles of His Word.

In addition, Jesus as the truth brings a deep sense of security and peace. In a world that is constantly changing, where truths are often questioned or redefined, Jesus remains the same—yesterday, today, and forever (Hebrews 13:8). This constancy gives us a firm foundation to stand on, a truth that we can rely on in every situation. No matter what happens in the world around us, no matter how much uncertainty or chaos we face, we can hold on to the truth that is Jesus. His truth is a refuge in times of trouble, a guide in times of uncertainty, and a source of strength in times of weakness. It is the truth that anchors our souls and keeps us steady, even when everything else is falling apart.

Finally, recognizing Jesus as the truth means that we are called to share that truth with others. Just as Jesus came to reveal the truth to us, we are called to be witnesses of that truth to the world. We are called to live out the truth of the gospel in our daily lives, to speak the truth in love, and to point others to the truth that is found in Jesus alone. This is not always easy, especially in a world that often rejects absolute truth, but it is our calling as followers of Christ. We are called to be bearers of the truth, to shine the light of Jesus in the darkness, and to proclaim the good news of His truth to a world that is desperate for something real, something solid, something that will not fade away.

In conclusion, when Jesus declared Himself to be the truth, He was making a profound statement about His identity and His mission. He is the embodiment of truth, the living, breathing reality of all that is true, good, and holy. To know Jesus is to know the truth, and to follow Him is to walk in that truth. This truth is not just a concept; it is a person, and that person is Jesus Christ, the Savior of the world. When we embrace Jesus as the truth, we find freedom, peace, and a firm foundation for our lives. We are called to live in that truth, to let it shape and define us, and to share it with a world that is searching for something real, something lasting, something true.

Chapter 3 – The Skepticism of the World

In Pilate's question, "What is truth?" we see a reflection of the deep skepticism that pervades the world today, a skepticism that challenges the very notion of absolute truth. Just as Pilate stood before Jesus, the embodiment of truth, and questioned the reality of what He represented, many people today struggle with or outright reject the idea that there is such a thing as absolute truth. Instead, they prefer to embrace relativism, the belief that truth is flexible, changing, and subjective, something that can be molded to fit individual perspectives or cultural norms. This skepticism is not just a casual doubt; it is a profound and often defiant stance against the idea that there is a fixed, unchanging truth that applies to all people, in all places, at all times. It reflects a world that has become increasingly uncomfortable with the idea of absolutes, where the idea that something could be definitively right or wrong, true or false, is seen as outdated or oppressive.

This skepticism has deep roots in the human desire for autonomy and control. To accept absolute truth is to admit that there is a standard outside of ourselves that we are accountable to, a truth that does not bend to our will or preferences. It means acknowledging that there are limits to our understanding, that there is a reality greater than our own experiences and desires. But for many, this is a hard pill to swallow. The world has taught us to value personal freedom above all else, to believe that we are the masters of our own destinies, and that truth is something we create for ourselves. In this context, the idea of absolute truth is seen as a threat, something that restricts our freedom and challenges our autonomy. And so, like Pilate, people respond with skepticism, questioning whether such a truth can even exist.

But this skepticism comes with a cost. When we reject the idea of absolute truth, we are left without a firm foundation to stand on. If truth is relative, if it changes from person to person or culture to culture, then what can we truly rely on? What can we hold onto when everything around us is shifting and uncertain? This is the dilemma that the world faces today. In the absence of absolute truth, we are left with a void, a sense of uncertainty and confusion that permeates every aspect of life. Without a solid foundation, we are tossed about by the winds of opinion, by the latest trends and philosophies, never finding the peace and security that comes from knowing the truth.

This skepticism also breeds a deep sense of distrust. If there is no absolute truth, then how can we trust anything or anyone? How can we know what is real or true? This lack of trust erodes relationships, communities, and societies, leaving people isolated, cynical, and fearful. It leads to a world where truth is seen as a weapon to be wielded, rather than a foundation to build upon, where people are more interested in winning arguments than in seeking the truth. This skepticism creates division and discord, as people retreat into their own versions of truth, unwilling or unable to engage with others in meaningful dialogue. It fosters a culture of suspicion, where everyone is questioned and nothing is taken at face value.

Yet, despite this pervasive skepticism, there remains a deep longing for truth, for something real and solid that we can hold onto. This longing is evident in the way people search for meaning and purpose, in the questions they ask and the struggles they face. Deep down, we all want to know the truth, even if we are afraid of what it might reveal. We want to believe that there is something greater than ourselves, something that gives our lives meaning and direction. This is why the question "What is truth?" resonates so deeply—it is a question that speaks to the core of our existence, to our need for something stable and unchanging in a world that is constantly shifting.

The challenge, then, is to move beyond skepticism and open ourselves to the possibility of absolute truth. This requires humility, a willingness to admit that we do not have all the answers, that there is a reality greater than ourselves that we must seek out and submit to. It requires courage, the strength to confront the truth, even when it challenges our beliefs or forces us to change. And it requires faith, the belief that there is a truth that is worth seeking, a truth that can be found in the person of Jesus Christ, who declared, "I am the way, the truth, and the life" (John 14:6).

In a world filled with skepticism, this is the truth that stands firm, unchanging and eternal. It is the truth that offers hope and healing, that brings clarity in confusion and light in darkness. It is the truth that sets us free from the chains of relativism, from the endless cycle of doubt and despair. It is the truth that gives our lives meaning and purpose, that anchors us in the midst of the storm. This is the truth that Pilate stood before and questioned, the truth that many still question today. But it is also the truth that has the power to transform our lives, to bring us into a relationship with the living God, and to give us the peace and security that we so desperately seek.

In the end, the skepticism of the world is not something to be dismissed or ignored, but to be understood and addressed. It is a reflection of the deep struggles and fears that we all face, the desire for freedom and autonomy that often leads us away from the truth. But it is also an opportunity, a chance to engage with the world in a meaningful way, to offer the truth of Christ as the answer to the questions and doubts that so many people carry. It is a chance to show that truth is not something to be feared, but something to be embraced, that it is not a burden, but a gift, something that gives us life, purpose, and direction. In a world that is skeptical of absolute truth, we have the opportunity to be witnesses to the truth, to live it out in our lives, and to share it with others, offering hope and light in a world that so desperately needs it.

Chapter 4 – The Search for Truth

Pilate's question, "What is truth?" reflects a profound and universal human experience—the search for truth that lies deep within every person's heart. This question is not just a fleeting thought or a moment of curiosity; it represents a fundamental aspect of what it means to be human. Every person, whether they are aware of it or not, is on a journey to find something real, something solid, something true to hold onto in a world that often feels chaotic, confusing, and full of uncertainty. This search for truth is woven into the fabric of our souls. It is the drive that pushes us to ask the big questions: Why am I here? What is my purpose? What is the meaning of life? We long for answers that go beyond the surface, that penetrate the depths of our existence and provide a foundation upon which we can build our lives. We want to believe that there is more to life than what we see with our eyes, that there is a deeper reality that gives meaning and purpose to everything we experience.

This search for truth is not always easy. It often takes us through dark and difficult places, forcing us to confront our doubts, fears, and insecurities. We may find ourselves questioning everything we once believed, wondering if anything can be truly known or trusted. The world offers us countless options, from philosophies to religions to ideologies, each claiming to hold the key to truth. But as we explore these different paths, we may find that many of them leave us feeling more lost and confused than before. They may offer temporary comfort or a sense of direction, but they often fail to satisfy the deep longing in our hearts for something that is real, lasting, and unchanging.

Yet, despite the challenges, the search for truth is one of the most important journeys we can undertake. It is a journey that shapes who we are and who we become. It forces us to dig deep, to question, to seek, and to wrestle with the big questions of life. And while the search for truth can be daunting, it is also incredibly rewarding. For those who persevere, who refuse to settle for easy answers or superficial beliefs, the search for truth can lead to a discovery that changes everything. It can lead us to a truth that is not just an idea or a concept, but a person—Jesus Christ. In Him, we find the truth we have been searching for, the truth that satisfies our deepest longings and gives us a firm foundation to stand on.

The search for truth is also a deeply personal journey. It is not something that can be done for us by someone else; it is a path we must walk ourselves. It requires us to be honest with ourselves, to acknowledge our doubts and questions, and to be willing to go wherever the truth may lead us. It requires courage, humility, and a willingness to let go of our preconceived notions and be open to new possibilities. This is not an easy task, especially in a world that often values certainty and quick answers over the slow, sometimes painful process of searching for truth. But for those who are willing to embark on this journey, the rewards are immeasurable.

As we search for truth, we are reminded that we are not alone in our quest. Throughout history, countless others have asked the same questions, faced the same doubts, and embarked on the same journey. The search for truth is a shared human experience, one that connects us to others and to the generations that have come before us. It is a journey that transcends time and place, a journey that unites us in our common humanity. And while the paths we take may be different, the destination is the same—the desire to find something real, something true, something that gives our lives meaning and purpose.

The search for truth also challenges us to look beyond ourselves. It reminds us that truth is not something we can create or control, but something that exists outside of us, something we must seek and discover. It calls us to be open to the possibility that the truth may be different from what we expect or want it to be. This requires a level of humility and surrender, a recognition that we do not have all the answers and that we need guidance and help along the way. It also requires us to be willing to change, to allow the truth to transform us and shape us into the people we are meant to be.

In the end, the search for truth is not just about finding answers, but about finding ourselves. It is about discovering who we are in relation to the truth, about finding our place in the world and our purpose in life. It is about building a life that is grounded in reality, in what is real and true, rather than in illusions or falsehoods. And while the journey may be long and difficult, it is ultimately a journey worth taking, for it leads us to a place of peace, fulfillment, and understanding.

Pilate's question, "What is truth?" serves as a reminder that the search for truth is a central part of the human experience. It is a journey that each of us must take, a journey that requires us to be honest, courageous, and open to the truth. It is a journey that leads us to the discovery of something real, something solid, something that gives our lives meaning and purpose. And for those who are willing to seek the truth with all their heart, they will find that the truth is not just an abstract concept or a set of ideas, but a person—Jesus Christ—who is the way, the truth, and the life. In Him, we find the answers to our deepest questions, the fulfillment of our deepest longings, and the foundation upon which we can build our lives. The search for truth is not just a quest for knowledge, but a journey of the heart, a journey that leads us to the source of all truth, to the One who is truth itself.

Chapter 5 – The Sense of Moral Responsibility

The question "What is truth?" asked by Pilate reveals a deep and challenging reality about the human condition—understanding the truth comes with a profound sense of moral responsibility. This is not just about knowing what is right and wrong, but about feeling the weight of that knowledge and understanding that once we know the truth, we are compelled to act upon it. There is a tension that arises between the clarity of truth and the obligation it imposes on us. Truth is not just a collection of facts or information; it is something that demands a response, a commitment to live in accordance with what we know to be right. Pilate, when faced with the truth embodied in Jesus Christ, felt this tension acutely. He knew, deep down, that Jesus was innocent, that He had done nothing deserving of death. Yet, Pilate found himself caught between the truth and the pressures of his position, the expectations of the crowd, and the fear of losing his own power. Instead of embracing the moral responsibility that came with the truth he recognized, Pilate chose to sidestep it. He tried to wash his hands of the situation, hoping to absolve himself of the consequences of the truth he could not deny. But truth cannot be so easily dismissed. The act of washing his hands was a symbolic attempt to escape the moral weight of his decision, but it did not remove the truth or the responsibility that came with it.

This tension between knowing the truth and the responsibility to act on it is something we all face in our lives. When we are confronted with the truth—whether it is about ourselves, our actions, or the world around us—we cannot simply ignore it or pretend it does not exist. The truth demands something from us; it calls us to respond, to make a choice, and to live in a way that reflects what we know to be true. This is not always easy. The truth can be uncomfortable, challenging, and even painful. It can force us to confront parts of ourselves that we would rather keep hidden, or to take actions that are difficult and costly. But ignoring the truth, or trying to evade the responsibility it brings, only leads to greater inner turmoil and a sense of being disconnected from what is real and true.

Pilate's attempt to distance himself from the truth is a reflection of a common human reaction to the weight of moral responsibility. We often want to find a way out, to avoid making the hard decisions that truth requires of us. We may rationalize our actions, shift the blame, or convince ourselves that it is not our problem to solve. But the truth remains, and with it, the responsibility to act in accordance with it. The more we try to avoid this responsibility, the more we find ourselves entangled in a web of compromise and self-deception. This is the danger of not facing the truth head-on—it leads us down a path where we become increasingly disconnected from our own sense of integrity and from the reality of the world around us.

At its core, the tension between truth and moral responsibility is about integrity. It is about being true to what we know, to the values we hold, and to the principles that guide our lives. When we compromise on the truth, we compromise on ourselves. We begin to lose our sense of who we are and what we stand for. This is why the decision to live according to the truth is so important. It is not just about doing the right thing; it is about maintaining our own sense of self, our own integrity, and our own connection to the world as it truly is.

The sense of moral responsibility that comes with knowing the truth also challenges us to be courageous. It takes courage to stand up for the truth, especially when it is unpopular, inconvenient, or comes with a personal cost. But courage is what allows us to live authentically and to be true to ourselves and to others. It is what enables us to take a stand, even when it is difficult, and to act with integrity in a world that often encourages compromise and falsehood.

Pilate's failure to embrace the moral responsibility of the truth before him serves as a cautionary tale. It shows us what can happen when we try to avoid the truth or shirk the responsibility that comes with it. Pilate's decision to wash his hands of the situation did not absolve him of responsibility; it only revealed his weakness and his unwillingness to stand up for what he knew was right. In the end, Pilate's name is forever associated with the act of surrendering the truth to the pressures of the world.

This is a powerful reminder that we, too, face moments in our lives where we must choose between the truth and the easier, more comfortable path of avoidance. The sense of moral responsibility that comes with truth is not a burden, but a call to live with integrity and purpose. It is an invitation to align our lives with what is real and true, to stand up for what is right, and to be people of character and courage. When we embrace this responsibility, we find a deeper sense of peace and fulfillment, knowing that we are living in accordance with the truth, no matter the cost.

In a world that often tries to blur the lines between right and wrong, truth and falsehood, the call to live with a sense of moral responsibility is more important than ever. It is what grounds us in reality, keeps us connected to our values, and guides us in making decisions that are not only right, but true. The tension between truth and responsibility may be challenging, but it is also what gives our lives meaning and direction. It is what allows us to live with integrity and to be a force for good in the world.

In conclusion, Pilate's question, "What is truth?" and his subsequent actions remind us that understanding the truth is only the first step. The real challenge lies in the moral responsibility that comes with that understanding. It calls us to be true to ourselves, to act with integrity, and to have the courage to stand up for what is right, even when it is difficult. The sense of moral responsibility is not something to be feared or avoided, but something to be embraced as a fundamental part of what it means to live a life of truth, purpose, and meaning.

Chapter 6 – The Stability of Truth in Injustice

In the midst of the darkest hour of human history, when Jesus stood before Pilate, the embodiment of truth was confronted with the depths of human injustice, corruption, and deceit. Pilate's questioning of truth during Jesus' trial is not just a moment frozen in time, but a profound lesson that echoes through the ages—truth is stable, unshakable, and stands firm even when surrounded by lies, injustice, and corruption. As Jesus, the innocent, blameless Son of God, was falsely accused, mocked, beaten, and condemned, the truth of His identity, His mission, and His divinity remained steadfast. No matter how many false witnesses were brought against Him, no matter how much the crowd clamored for His crucifixion, the truth did not waver. It was not altered by the lies that were told, nor was it diminished by the injustice of the trial. The truth of who Jesus was, and is, remained constant, shining brightly in the face of the darkness that sought to overcome it. This moment in history teaches us something crucial: that truth, real truth, does not bend or break under pressure. It does not change to fit the narrative of those in power, and it cannot be silenced by the voices of the many. Truth is like a rock, immovable and unchanging, even when the storms of injustice rage around it.

In our own lives, we are often confronted with situations where lies, deceit, and injustice seem to prevail. We see corruption in the world, we witness the innocent being punished, and the guilty walking free. It can be disheartening, making us question whether truth really matters, or if it can stand up to the power of falsehood. But the trial of Jesus reminds us that truth is not dependent on human circumstances. It is not swayed by the opinions of the masses, nor is it subject to the whims of those in authority. Truth exists independently of these things, and it endures even when everything around it is falling apart. When we look at the cross, we see the ultimate example of truth standing firm in the face of overwhelming injustice. Jesus, who is the way, the truth, and the life, was condemned to die not because the truth was weak, but because He was willing to bear the weight of the world's lies, sin, and corruption to reveal the power and stability of truth.

This teaches us that in a world full of injustice, where it often seems that falsehood is winning, we can find hope and strength in the knowledge that truth will ultimately prevail. It may not happen immediately, and it may not be in the way we expect, but truth cannot be destroyed. It is eternal, grounded in the very nature of God, who is Himself truth. This stability of truth is a foundation that we can stand on, a refuge in times of trouble. It gives us the courage to speak out against injustice, to stand up for what is right, even when it feels like we are standing alone. It reassures us that our efforts to live truthfully, to seek justice, and to act with integrity are not in vain, even if the world around us seems to be ruled by deceit and corruption.

Moreover, the stability of truth in the midst of injustice calls us to be people of truth in our own lives. It challenges us to live with integrity, to be honest in our dealings, and to refuse to compromise our principles, no matter the cost. It reminds us that truth is not just an abstract concept, but a way of life, a commitment to uphold what is right and just, even when it is difficult. This commitment to truth is what allows us to navigate a world that is often full of gray areas, where right and wrong are not always clear. It gives us a compass, a guide that helps us make decisions that are not only wise but just. It helps us to see beyond the immediate and the temporary, to understand that truth, in the end, will outlast all falsehoods and that justice will ultimately be served.

The example of Jesus standing before Pilate, silent in the face of false accusations, yet unwavering in His truth, is a powerful reminder that truth does not need to be defended by force or manipulation. It does not require us to shout louder than those who oppose it or to outmaneuver those who seek to distort it. Truth stands on its own, and its power is found not in its ability to conquer, but in its ability to endure. This endurance is what gives us hope when we face injustice in our own lives, whether it is personal, societal, or global. It reminds us that while lies may seem to flourish for a time, they are ultimately fleeting, like shadows that disappear in the light of the truth.

In this way, the stability of truth becomes a source of peace for us. We do not need to be anxious or fearful about the lies and injustices we see around us, because we know that truth will not be moved. It will not be overcome. It is a foundation that we can build our lives on, a solid ground that will not give way under pressure. This is the peace that comes from knowing that we are aligned with the truth, that we are living in accordance with what is real and right, and that no matter what happens in the world around us, the truth remains.

Ultimately, the stability of truth in the midst of injustice points us to the hope we have in Jesus Christ. His resurrection is the ultimate proof that truth cannot be defeated, that it will rise again, even from the darkest and most unjust circumstances.

This is the hope that sustains us, that gives us the strength to continue standing for truth, to continue seeking justice, and to continue living with integrity, no matter the cost. It is the hope that reminds us that in the end, truth will prevail, and justice will be done.

In conclusion, Pilate's questioning of truth during Jesus' trial is a powerful lesson that truth is stable and unchanging, even in the face of lies, injustice, and corruption. It teaches us that truth does not shift or bend under pressure, that it remains firm and reliable, no matter the circumstances. This stability of truth is our foundation, our refuge, and our hope. It calls us to live with integrity, to stand up for what is right, and to trust that truth, in the end, will prevail. In a world where injustice often seems to reign, the stability of truth gives us the courage to keep standing, to keep speaking, and to keep believing in the power of what is right, knowing that truth will never be overcome.

Chapter 7 – The Struggle to Accept Truth

Pilate's question, "What is truth?" followed by his actions, reveals a deep and universal human struggle—the struggle to accept or act on the truth, especially when it challenges our deeply held beliefs or threatens our position. This struggle is not unique to Pilate; it is something that each of us experiences at different points in our lives. There is a natural human tendency to resist or suppress the truth when it forces us to confront uncomfortable realities, when it challenges the narratives we have built around ourselves, or when it threatens the status quo that we rely on for our sense of security and identity. Pilate, standing before the truth embodied in Jesus Christ, felt the weight of this struggle acutely. He knew that Jesus was innocent, that the charges against Him were baseless, and that the truth was standing right in front of him. Yet, despite this knowledge, Pilate could not bring himself to act on the truth. The pressure from the crowd, the fear of losing his position, and the desire to maintain political stability all conspired against the truth, leading Pilate to wash his hands of the matter, hoping to absolve himself of the responsibility that truth demands. But truth, once known, cannot be so easily dismissed or ignored. It lingers in our conscience, a constant reminder that we are called to act with integrity, even when it is difficult, even when it costs us something.

This struggle to accept truth is something we all face. It is rooted in our fear of change, our fear of loss, and our fear of the unknown. The truth often requires us to let go of the illusions we have clung to, to step out of our comfort zones, and to confront the parts of ourselves that we would rather keep hidden. It demands honesty, vulnerability, and a willingness to be transformed. But these demands can be terrifying. It is much easier to stay in denial, to justify our actions, or to convince ourselves that the truth is not as clear as it seems. We create elaborate defenses to protect ourselves from the truth, to keep it at arm's length, because deep down, we know that accepting the truth means that something will have to change. And change is hard. It is uncomfortable. It is often painful. Yet, without the willingness to accept the truth, we remain stuck, unable to grow, unable to move forward, trapped in a cycle of self-deception and avoidance.

Pilate's actions—his reluctance to act on the truth—mirror this common human experience. Faced with the truth, he hesitated, he wavered, he sought a way out that would allow him to avoid the consequences of standing up for what was right. He allowed the fear of the crowd, the fear of losing his position, and the fear of political instability to cloud his judgment, to suppress the voice of truth that was speaking clearly to him. In doing so, Pilate chose the path of least resistance, the path that allowed him to maintain his position and avoid conflict, but at the cost of his integrity and his conscience. This is a powerful reminder of how easy it is to fall into the same trap—how easy it is to prioritize our comfort, our security, and our position over the truth.

Yet, the truth, no matter how much we try to suppress it, has a way of resurfacing. It does not simply disappear because we choose to ignore it. It remains, like a quiet but persistent voice, reminding us that we are not living in alignment with what we know to be true. This internal conflict can manifest in many ways—through feelings of guilt, anxiety, or a sense of emptiness. We may try to fill this void with distractions, with rationalizations, or with more denial, but the truth remains, waiting for us to have the courage to face it, to accept it, and to act on it.

The struggle to accept the truth is not just about big, life-altering decisions. It is something that can happen in the small, everyday moments of our lives as well. It can be as simple as admitting when we are wrong, acknowledging a mistake, or being honest about our feelings. It can be about recognizing when we are holding onto a belief or a habit that no longer serves us, or when we are staying in a situation that is not healthy or right. In these moments, the struggle to accept the truth can feel just as intense as it did for Pilate, because it requires us to confront ourselves, to be honest about who we are and where we need to grow.

However, the act of accepting the truth, difficult as it may be, is ultimately liberating. When we choose to face the truth, to embrace it, and to act on it, we open the door to growth, healing, and transformation. We free ourselves from the burden of denial, from the weight of living a lie, and we step into the light of reality, where we can see clearly and move forward with integrity. Accepting the truth allows us to live authentically, to align our actions with our values, and to build a life that is grounded in what is real and true.

In the end, Pilate's struggle to accept the truth is a mirror that reflects our own struggles. It challenges us to ask ourselves: Where in our lives are we resisting the truth? Where are we choosing comfort over integrity? Where are we allowing fear to keep us from acting on what we know is right? And most importantly, how can we find the courage to accept the truth, even when it is hard, even when it requires us to change, even when it threatens our position or our sense of security?

The struggle to accept the truth is a part of the human experience, but it is not the end of the story. By recognizing this struggle and choosing to face it, we take the first step toward living a life of integrity, a life that is aligned with the truth, a life that is free from the chains of self-deception and avoidance. It is a journey that requires courage, honesty, and a willingness to be transformed. But it is a journey worth taking, because in the end, the truth will set us free. And in that freedom, we find the peace, the fulfillment, and the sense of purpose that can only come from living in alignment with what is true.

Chapter 8 – The Seriousness of Ignoring Truth

The story of Pilate and his failure to recognize and act on the truth is a sobering reminder of the serious, even tragic, consequences that can result when we choose to ignore or sideline the truth. Pilate stood face to face with the truth embodied in Jesus Christ, yet in that critical moment, he chose to wash his hands of the matter, to step back from the responsibility that truth demands. He knew that Jesus was innocent, that the accusations against Him were baseless, but instead of standing up for what was right, Pilate allowed fear, political pressure, and the desire to maintain his position to cloud his judgment. His decision to ignore the truth did not just affect him—it led to the crucifixion of an innocent man, an act of unimaginable injustice that has echoed through history. This is not just a historical event; it is a powerful lesson for all of us. It shows us that when we choose to ignore the truth, when we sideline it in favor of convenience, comfort, or self-preservation, we are not just making a simple mistake—we are setting the stage for serious and often tragic consequences.

Ignoring the truth is never a neutral act. It is a decision that has ripple effects, impacting not just ourselves but those around us. When we turn a blind eye to the truth, we create a space for lies, deceit, and injustice to take root and grow. We allow falsehood to flourish, and in doing so, we contribute to a culture where truth becomes secondary, where what is right is overshadowed by what is expedient. Pilate's decision to ignore the truth led to the death of Jesus, but the consequences of ignoring the truth are not always so immediately visible. Sometimes they unfold slowly, over time, as the effects of our choices compound and spread. But whether the consequences are immediate or delayed, they are always serious. When we choose to ignore the truth, we undermine the very foundation of integrity, justice, and trust that our lives and societies are built upon.

The seriousness of ignoring the truth is evident in every aspect of life. In our personal lives, ignoring the truth can lead to broken relationships, lost opportunities, and a sense of deep regret. It can cause us to live in denial, to build our lives on shaky ground, and to distance ourselves from the reality that we must face in order to grow and heal. In our professional lives, ignoring the truth can lead to unethical decisions, corruption, and a loss of credibility and respect. It can damage our reputation, our career, and our ability to lead and inspire others. In our communities and societies, ignoring the truth can lead to injustice, oppression, and the breakdown of trust and cooperation. It can create an environment where lies are accepted as truth, where power is abused, and where those who are most vulnerable are left to suffer the consequences of our inaction.

But the consequences of ignoring the truth are not just external—they are also internal. When we ignore the truth, we are forced to live with the knowledge that we have compromised our integrity, that we have chosen to turn away from what is right. This creates an internal conflict, a sense of guilt, shame, and unease that can weigh heavily on our hearts and minds. It erodes our sense of self-worth, our confidence, and our peace of mind. We may try to justify our actions, to convince ourselves that we had no choice, or that it was the best decision at the time, but deep down, we know that we have betrayed not just the truth, but ourselves.

The story of Pilate is a warning to all of us. It reminds us that the truth is not something to be taken lightly or brushed aside. It is a powerful force that demands our respect, our attention, and our action. When we are faced with the truth, we have a responsibility to recognize it, to act on it, and to stand up for it, even when it is difficult, even when it comes at a cost. The consequences of ignoring the truth are too serious to ignore. They are not just about the immediate impact of our decisions, but about the long-term effects on our character, our relationships, and our society.

Ignoring the truth can lead to a life filled with regret, with missed opportunities to do what is right, to make a difference, to stand up for justice. It can lead to a life where we are constantly looking over our shoulder, wondering when the truth we have ignored will catch up with us. It can lead to a life where we are disconnected from the people and the principles that matter most, where we are living a lie rather than embracing the truth.

But there is hope. The story of Pilate also teaches us that it is never too late to choose the truth. While Pilate's decision had tragic consequences, we have the opportunity to learn from his mistake, to choose a different path. We can choose to face the truth, to embrace it, and to let it guide our decisions and our actions. We can choose to stand up for what is right, to speak out against injustice, and to live with integrity, even when it is difficult, even when it costs us something.

The truth is not always easy to face, but it is always worth it. It is the foundation of a life well-lived, a life that is grounded in reality, in what is right and just. It is the foundation of relationships built on trust, of communities built on cooperation and respect, of societies built on justice and equality. The truth is the foundation of our integrity, our character, and our sense of self-worth. When we choose to ignore the truth, we are not just making a mistake—we are undermining the very foundation of our lives.

In conclusion, Pilate's failure to recognize and act on the truth is a powerful reminder of the seriousness of ignoring or sidelining the truth. It shows us that the consequences of ignoring the truth are not just immediate, but long-lasting, affecting every aspect of our lives. It challenges us to face the truth, to act on it, and to stand up for what is right, no matter the cost. It reminds us that the truth is a powerful force that demands our respect and our action, and that the consequences of ignoring it are too serious to ignore. It is a lesson that we must take to heart, a lesson that can guide us as we navigate the complexities of life, as we seek to live with integrity, and as we strive to make a difference in the world.

Chapter 9 – The Standard of Character

Pilate's interaction with Jesus during that fateful trial stands as a powerful testament to the idea that truth is not just an abstract concept but a profound standard of character. In that moment, Pilate was not merely a Roman governor deciding the fate of a man accused by the crowd; he was a human being faced with a choice that would define who he was at his core. He stood at a crossroads where he had to choose between doing what was politically expedient—maintaining his position, appeasing the angry crowd, and avoiding potential unrest—or standing up for the truth that he knew in his heart. Jesus, an innocent man, stood before him, embodying the truth with a calmness and dignity that must have struck Pilate deeply. Pilate knew the charges against Jesus were false, that the man before him was not deserving of death. The truth was clear, yet the weight of the decision was crushing. In that critical moment, Pilate's choice would reveal the true measure of his character, not just as a leader but as a man.

The standard of character that truth demands is not something that can be easily bypassed or ignored. It calls us to rise above our fears, our desires for self-preservation, and our inclinations to take the path of least resistance. It challenges us to act with integrity, even when doing so is difficult or comes with a cost. For Pilate, this cost was immense. To stand up for the truth would have meant going against the will of the crowd, risking his position, and possibly inciting a riot that could jeopardize his career and his life. The easier path was clear—wash his hands of the situation, literally and figuratively, and let the people have their way. But in choosing the easier path, Pilate compromised not just his role as a judge but his very character. He revealed that when faced with a choice between truth and self-interest, he was willing to sacrifice the former for the latter.

This moment in Pilate's life teaches us that the choices we make when confronted with the truth are not just about the situations at hand; they are about who we are and who we become. Each decision we make, each time we choose whether to stand up for what is right or to take the easy way out, we are shaping our character. We are building the person we are, brick by brick, decision by decision. And it is in these moments of decision, when the stakes are high and the pressure is on, that our true character is revealed. For Pilate, the decision to hand Jesus over to be crucified, despite knowing the truth of His innocence, marked him forever. It was a decision that exposed the weakness in his character, a willingness to bend to the pressures of the world rather than stand firm on the foundation of truth.

But Pilate's story is not just a cautionary tale; it is a mirror that reflects our own lives. How often do we find ourselves in situations where standing up for the truth requires us to go against the grain, to face potential backlash, or to sacrifice something valuable? How often do we, like Pilate, feel the weight of the world's expectations pressing down on us, tempting us to compromise our values, our integrity, and our commitment to what is right? And how often do we, in those moments, find ourselves faltering, choosing the path of least resistance rather than the path of truth? Pilate's decision challenges us to examine our own character, to ask ourselves whether we have the courage to stand up for the truth, even when it is difficult, even when it costs us something.

The standard of character that truth demands is not about perfection; it is about consistency and integrity. It is about being true to what we know is right, even when no one is watching, even when the world is telling us to do otherwise. It is about having the strength to say no to what is wrong and yes to what is right, regardless of the consequences. This standard is not something that we can achieve overnight; it is something that we build over time, through the choices we make, the actions we take, and the principles we live by. It is a standard that is forged in the fires of adversity, tested in the crucible of difficult decisions, and strengthened by the resolve to live with integrity.

For Pilate, the choice he made that day revealed a character that was lacking in strength, courage, and conviction. It showed a man who was more concerned with maintaining his position and avoiding conflict than with upholding the truth and justice. It revealed a man who, when faced with the ultimate test of character, chose to sacrifice his integrity for the sake of expediency. And in doing so, Pilate lost more than just his integrity; he lost the respect of history, becoming forever associated with the betrayal of truth and justice.

But Pilate's failure does not have to be our own. We have the opportunity to learn from his mistakes, to choose a different path, to build our character on the foundation of truth rather than on the shifting sands of convenience and self-interest. We have the chance to be people of integrity, who stand up for what is right, who live by the standard of truth, and who are not swayed by the pressures of the world. This is not an easy path, but it is the path that leads to true fulfillment, respect, and a legacy that we can be proud of.

In conclusion, Pilate's interaction with Jesus is a powerful reminder that truth is a standard of character, one that challenges us to rise above our fears and self-interest, to act with integrity, and to stand up for what is right, no matter the cost. It is a reminder that the choices we make when confronted with the truth reveal the true measure of our character. Pilate's decision to ignore the truth and to choose expediency over integrity is a cautionary tale, but it is also an opportunity for us to reflect on our own lives and to commit to living by the standard of truth, to being people of character who choose what is right, even when it is difficult. It is a call to build our lives on the solid foundation of truth, to live with integrity, and to be the kind of people who, when faced with the ultimate test of character, choose to stand firm on the side of truth.

Chapter 10 – The Supremacy of Truth

The question "What is truth?" posed by Pilate over two thousand years ago, continues to echo through the corridors of time, resonating with the same urgency and relevance today as it did then. This question cuts to the very heart of human existence, challenging us to confront the nature of reality and our place within it. The supremacy of truth is a concept that transcends the limitations of time, culture, and human opinion. It is not something that can be molded to fit our preferences, nor can it be altered by the shifting sands of societal trends. Truth stands supreme, eternal, and unchanging, like a beacon of light in a world often shrouded in darkness. It is the foundation upon which everything else is built, the cornerstone of a life lived with integrity, purpose, and meaning. Throughout history, empires have risen and fallen, cultures have come and gone, but the truth remains steadfast, unwavering in its essence. It is a force that cannot be silenced, a reality that cannot be ignored, no matter how much the world may try to distort or suppress it. The enduring relevance of Jesus' teachings is perhaps the most powerful testament to the supremacy of truth. His words, spoken in a time and place far removed from our own, continue to speak to the deepest needs of the human heart, offering guidance, comfort, and challenge in equal measure. Jesus declared, "I am the way, the truth, and the life" (John 14:6), a statement that not only affirms the existence of absolute truth but also establishes its source in Him.

The supremacy of truth means that it is not subject to the whims of human interpretation or the pressures of popular opinion. It is not something that can be voted on, debated, or negotiated. Truth exists independently of our understanding or acceptance of it. It is a reality that we must align ourselves with, rather than something we can bend to suit our desires. This is a humbling realization, for it reminds us that there are absolutes in the universe, principles that govern life, morality, and the very fabric of existence, whether we acknowledge them or not. The supremacy of truth calls us to a higher standard, one that requires us to seek, embrace, and live according to what is real and true, even when it is inconvenient, uncomfortable, or counter to the prevailing culture.

In a world where relativism often reigns, where truth is seen as fluid, personal, and subjective, the concept of absolute truth can be both challenging and liberating. It challenges us because it confronts the idea that we can each create our own truth, that what is true for one person may not be true for another. The supremacy of truth reminds us that there is a reality that exists beyond our personal experiences, opinions, and beliefs, a reality that we are called to discover and align ourselves with. At the same time, this understanding is liberating because it offers a solid foundation in a world that often feels unstable and uncertain. When everything else is shifting and changing, truth remains a constant, a reliable guide that can lead us through the complexities of life.

The supremacy of truth is also a call to integrity. It demands that we live in a way that is consistent with what we know to be true. This means being honest with ourselves and others, standing up for what is right, even when it is difficult, and refusing to compromise our principles for the sake of convenience or gain. It is about living authentically, with a clear conscience, knowing that our actions align with the truth. This is not always easy, especially in a world that often rewards deceit, manipulation, and compromise. But the supremacy of truth gives us the courage to stand firm, to hold fast to our values, and to trust that, in the end, truth will prevail.

The enduring relevance of Jesus' teachings is a powerful example of the supremacy of truth. His words have transcended time, culture, and circumstance, continuing to inspire, challenge, and transform lives across generations. The truths He taught about love, forgiveness, justice, and humility are as relevant today as they were two thousand years ago. They speak to the universal human experience, addressing the deepest needs and longings of the human heart. This enduring relevance is a testament to the fact that truth is not bound by time or culture; it is eternal and unchanging. It is a reality that we can build our lives upon, a foundation that will never crumble or fade away.

The supremacy of truth also calls us to humility. It reminds us that we do not have all the answers, that our understanding is limited, and that we must approach the truth with a spirit of openness and a willingness to learn. It challenges us to seek the truth with diligence and integrity, to question our assumptions, and to be willing to change when confronted with new insights or understanding. This humility is essential if we are to grow and mature in our understanding of the world and our place in it. It allows us to engage with others in a spirit of respect and dialogue, recognizing that we are all on a journey of discovery and that the truth is something we pursue together.

In conclusion, the question "What is truth?" is not just a philosophical inquiry; it is a question that strikes at the very core of our existence. The supremacy of truth means that it is not bound by time, culture, or human opinion. It is eternal, unchanging, and absolute. It is a reality that we must align ourselves with if we are to live lives of integrity, purpose, and meaning. The enduring relevance of Jesus' teachings is a powerful testament to this truth, offering us a guide that transcends time and circumstance. In a world that often seems chaotic and uncertain, the supremacy of truth provides us with a solid foundation, a constant that we can rely on. It challenges us to live with integrity, to seek the truth with humility, and to trust that, in the end, truth will prevail. The supremacy of truth is a call to live authentically, to stand up for what is right, and to build our lives on the unshakable foundation of what is real and true. It is a call to recognize that truth is not something we create, but something we discover, embrace, and live by. It is a call to live in alignment with the reality that transcends us, a reality that offers us the hope, guidance, and stability we need in a world that is often anything but stable.

Chapter 11 – The Submission to Truth

Pilate's question, "What is truth?" was met with silence from Jesus, yet that silence was louder than any answer could have been. The truth of Jesus' identity stood before Pilate, undeniable and profound, a truth so powerful that it did not need to be spoken because it was already evident. This moment teaches us that truth is not something we can merely contemplate or debate from a distance; it is something that demands a response, a choice, a decision that reflects the core of who we are. Truth requires submission, and whether we accept it or reject it, we cannot remain neutral in its presence. This is because truth, by its very nature, confronts us. It challenges the illusions we have built, the lies we have told ourselves, and the comfortable beliefs that shield us from reality. When we are faced with the truth, we stand at a crossroads where neutrality is not an option. To ignore the truth, to pretend it does not exist, is to make a choice just as much as to embrace it. Pilate's indecision, his attempt to wash his hands of the situation, was itself a decision—a decision to avoid the truth, to evade the responsibility that truth carries, and in doing so, to align himself with falsehood.

This lesson is vital for all of us because we often find ourselves in situations where the truth is clear, yet inconvenient, uncomfortable, or even frightening. We might be tempted to delay, to sidestep, or to rationalize our inaction, thinking that by doing nothing, we are remaining neutral. But the truth remains, unchanged and unyielding, and our failure to submit to it only deepens the consequences of our avoidance. Truth, when it is revealed, shines a light on everything hidden, exposing the reality that we must face. It does not allow for half-measures or partial acceptance. We are called to either submit to the truth, allowing it to shape our actions, decisions, and lives, or to reject it, which inevitably leads us down a path of self-deception and inner conflict.

The requirement of submission to truth is not about losing our freedom or being forced into something against our will. Rather, it is about recognizing that truth is the foundation upon which a meaningful, authentic life is built. When we submit to truth, we are aligning ourselves with what is real, what is just, and what is good. This submission is not a sign of weakness, but of strength, courage, and integrity. It takes strength to admit when we are wrong, to change course when we have been heading in the wrong direction, and to live according to the principles that truth demands. It takes courage to stand up for what is true, especially when it goes against the grain of popular opinion, societal pressures, or personal desires. And it takes integrity to remain consistent in our commitment to truth, even when it costs us something.

Pilate's failure to submit to the truth of Jesus' innocence and divine identity shows us the dangers of refusing to acknowledge and act upon the truth. By trying to remain neutral, Pilate ended up complicit in the greatest injustice in history. His choice to avoid the truth, rather than to embrace it, led to tragic consequences that could have been avoided had he chosen to stand by what he knew was right. This teaches us that our choices in the face of truth are not just about the immediate situation—they are about who we are becoming and the legacy we are leaving behind. When we choose to submit to truth, we are choosing to live with integrity, to be people who stand by what is right, no matter the cost. When we reject the truth, we are choosing a path that ultimately leads to regret, guilt, and a loss of our own sense of self.

Submission to truth also involves humility. It requires us to admit that we do not have all the answers, that we are not the ultimate authority in our lives, and that there is a higher standard that we must adhere to. This humility is not about diminishing ourselves, but about placing ourselves in the proper relationship to the truth. It is about acknowledging that truth exists independently of our opinions, desires, or perceptions, and that our task is to discover, understand, and align ourselves with it. This alignment brings clarity, peace, and purpose to our lives, as we are no longer living in conflict with reality, but in harmony with it.

Furthermore, submission to truth is a lifelong journey. It is not a one-time decision, but a daily commitment to seek the truth, to live by it, and to allow it to transform us. This journey requires ongoing reflection, self-examination, and a willingness to grow and change. It calls us to be honest with ourselves about where we are falling short, where we are resisting the truth, and where we need to make adjustments in our lives. It is a journey that demands perseverance, as the truth is not always easy to live out, especially in a world that often values convenience, comfort, and compromise over integrity and justice.

In conclusion, Pilate's unanswered question, "What is truth?" serves as a powerful reminder that truth is not something we can remain neutral about. It demands a response, a choice, and ultimately, submission. Whether we accept the truth or reject it, we are making a decision that will shape our character, our actions, and our future. Submission to truth is not about losing our freedom, but about finding the strength, courage, and integrity to live in alignment with what is real and just. It is about recognizing that truth is the foundation of a meaningful life and choosing to build our lives on that solid foundation. Pilate's failure to submit to the truth shows us the dangers of trying to evade or ignore the truth, and the tragic consequences that can result from such a decision. In contrast, when we choose to submit to the truth, we are choosing a path of integrity, clarity, and purpose, a path that leads to true freedom and fulfillment. The journey of submission to truth is challenging, but it is also deeply rewarding, as it allows us to live authentically, to grow in wisdom and understanding, and to contribute to a world where truth, justice, and goodness prevail.

Chapter 12 – The Steadfastness of Truth

Pilate's question, "What is truth?" captures the deep confusion that has plagued humanity for centuries—a confusion that seems to grow more intense as the world becomes increasingly complex and fragmented. In a time when truth is often skewed, distorted, and manipulated to serve various agendas, it's easy to feel lost, uncertain, and overwhelmed. We live in a world where information is abundant, but clarity is scarce, where voices clamor for attention, each claiming to offer the truth, yet leaving us more confused than ever. The very concept of truth has been stretched and twisted, often treated as a mere tool to achieve power, influence, or validation rather than as an absolute standard to live by. This confusion isn't just an intellectual dilemma; it's a deeply emotional and spiritual one. It touches every part of our lives, from the decisions we make to the beliefs we hold, from the relationships we form to the sense of purpose we carry within us. In such a world, where do we turn? How do we find something real, something solid, something true to hold onto? This is where the steadfastness of truth, as revealed in Jesus Christ, becomes not just a beacon of hope but an anchor for our souls.

Amidst the swirling chaos of conflicting ideas, ideologies, and interpretations, Jesus stands as the unwavering, unchanging revelation of truth. His life, His teachings, and His very being are the embodiment of truth in its purest form—a truth that is not subject to the whims of culture, the distortions of power, or the biases of human understanding. Jesus declared, "I am the way, the truth, and the life" (John 14:6), and in that declaration, He offered us a lifeline in a world drowning in confusion. He didn't just speak the truth; He lived it, He embodied it, and He revealed it in every word, every action, and every sacrifice. In a world where truth is often seen as relative or subjective, Jesus presents a truth that is absolute, eternal, and deeply personal—a truth that doesn't just inform our minds but transforms our hearts and lives.

The steadfastness of truth in Jesus is a profound source of comfort and guidance for those who seek it with a sincere heart. It offers us a foundation that remains firm, even when everything else around us is shifting and uncertain. When we are bombarded with conflicting messages, when we are unsure of what to believe or who to trust, we can turn to Jesus, knowing that His truth is unshakable, that it will guide us through the fog of confusion and lead us to clarity and peace. This truth is not hidden or elusive; it is revealed to all who are willing to seek it, to open their hearts and minds to it, and to let it shape their lives. Jesus' truth cuts through the noise, the lies, and the half-truths that so often dominate our world, offering us a clear, direct path to understanding, wisdom, and meaning.

In this steadfastness, there is also a deep sense of security. We live in a time when so much feels unstable—economies fluctuate, political systems are in turmoil, and the very fabric of society seems to be fraying at the edges. Yet, in the midst of all this instability, the truth of Jesus remains a rock that we can stand on, a refuge where we can find safety and assurance. It tells us that no matter how much the world changes, no matter how much uncertainty we face, there is something that remains constant, reliable, and true. This steadfast truth is not just an abstract concept; it is a living reality that we can experience, a relationship with Jesus that grounds us, centers us, and gives us the strength to face whatever comes our way.

Moreover, the steadfastness of truth in Jesus calls us to be steadfast in our own lives. It challenges us to live with integrity, to stand firm in our convictions, and to be true to what we know is right, even when the world around us is pulling us in different directions. It reminds us that truth is not something that can be compromised or watered down to fit our desires or the expectations of others. Truth demands commitment, perseverance, and courage. It calls us to be people of character, who are not swayed by the winds of change or the pressures of society but who remain faithful to the truth, no matter the cost.

This steadfast truth also brings hope. In a world that often feels bleak, where injustice, suffering, and deceit seem to have the upper hand, the truth of Jesus assures us that goodness, justice, and love will ultimately prevail. It reminds us that the confusion of the world is temporary, that the darkness cannot overcome the light, and that the truth will, in the end, triumph over all falsehood. This hope is not just wishful thinking; it is rooted in the reality of who Jesus is and what He has done. His resurrection is the ultimate proof that truth cannot be defeated, that it is stronger than death, stronger than sin, stronger than any force that seeks to undermine it.

In conclusion, Pilate's question, "What is truth?" reflects the deep confusion that so many of us feel in a world where truth is often distorted and hard to find. But in Jesus, we find the steadfast revelation of truth, a truth that remains unchanging and reliable, guiding those who seek it with a sincere heart. This truth is a source of comfort, security, and guidance in a world full of uncertainty and confusion. It calls us to live with integrity, to stand firm in our convictions, and to trust that the truth will ultimately prevail. The steadfastness of Jesus' truth is not just a concept to be believed; it is a reality to be lived, a relationship to be embraced, and a foundation to be built upon. In a world where everything else may fail, the truth of Jesus remains, unshakable and eternal, offering us the clarity, direction, and hope we need to navigate the complexities of life.

Conclusion

As we reach the conclusion of "What Is Truth? - From Skepticism to Submission," we return to the haunting question posed by Pilate in John 18:38: "What is truth?" This question, asked in the presence of Jesus Christ—who boldly declared, "Jesus saith unto him, I am the way, the truth, and the life" (John 14:6)—captures the tension between human skepticism and the divine revelation of truth. Pilate, standing before Truth incarnate, chose to dismiss the answer that stood right before him. He was confronted with the opportunity to embrace the ultimate truth but instead chose the path of political expediency and moral compromise. Pilate's failure to submit to the truth is a cautionary tale, one that holds profound relevance for us today.

Throughout this book, we have explored the journey from skepticism to submission—a journey that challenges us to confront the truth, not as an abstract concept, but as a living reality embodied in the person of Jesus Christ. We have seen how society, much like Pilate, often struggles with the idea of absolute truth, preferring the comfort of relativism and the illusion of personal autonomy. Yet, as we have learned, truth is not something that can be molded to fit our desires; it is an unchanging standard by which we are called to live. The truth of Jesus Christ demands a response, and that response must go beyond intellectual acknowledgment—it must lead to a life of submission, a life that is aligned with the reality of who He is.

As we conclude, the challenge before us is clear: How will we continue to walk in the truth that has been revealed to us? How will we allow the lessons shared in these pages to shape our daily lives, our decisions, and our relationships? The journey from skepticism to submission is not a one-time event; it is a daily commitment to follow the way, the truth, and the life. It requires us to continually examine our hearts, to root out the doubts and fears that hinder our submission, and to embrace the truth of Jesus Christ with unwavering faith.

To walk in the truth means to live with integrity, to uphold the principles of God's Word in every area of our lives, and to reject the lies and deceptions that the world often presents as truth. It means being willing to stand firm in our convictions, even when it is difficult, even when it costs us something. But it also means living in the freedom and joy that come from knowing that we are walking in the light, that our lives are built on a foundation that cannot be shaken. As Jesus said, "And ye shall know the truth, and the truth shall make you free." (John 8:32). This freedom is not the freedom to do as we please, but the freedom to live as we were created to live—in alignment with the truth of God's design and purpose for our lives.

In the end, the journey from skepticism to submission is a journey of transformation. It is a journey that leads us away from the confusion and uncertainty of the world and into the clarity and peace of knowing the truth in Jesus Christ. As we continue in our walk with the Lord, let us commit ourselves to this path, to seek the truth with all our hearts, to submit to it with all our strength, and to live it out with all our lives. For in doing so, we will find the true meaning of what it means to live in the light of the truth, to experience the fullness of life that Jesus promised, and to stand firm in the face of whatever challenges may come our way. May we, unlike Pilate, recognize the truth before us and have the courage to submit to it, allowing it to guide us, shape us, and ultimately, transform us into the people God has called us to be.

Don't miss out!

Visit the website below and you can sign up to receive emails whenever Joshua Rhoades publishes a new book. There's no charge and no obligation.

https://books2read.com/r/B-A-AJLBB-CVLVE

BOOKS 2 READ

Connecting independent readers to independent writers.

Did you love *What Is Truth? - From Skepticism to Submission?* Then you should read *Sounding The Call - The Voice of Conviction*[1] by Joshua Rhoades!

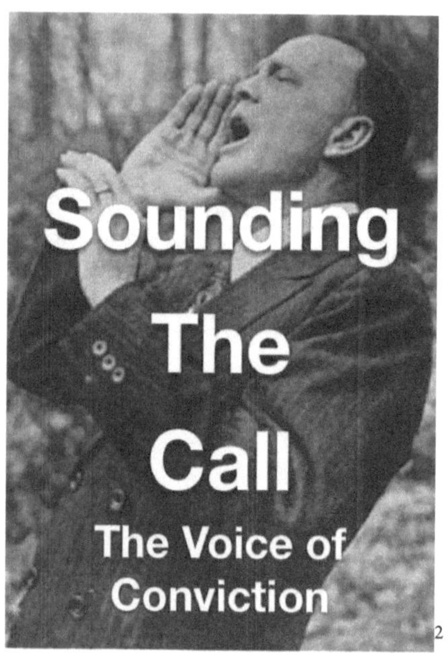

In a world filled with noise, where countless voices vie for our attention, the voice of conviction often stands out as a beacon of truth and clarity. This voice, rooted in the divine call to righteousness, echoes through the ages, urging humanity to confront sin, seek justice, and return to a life aligned with God's will. Isaiah 58:1 captures this urgency and powerfully encapsulates the role of the prophet: "Cry aloud, spare not, lift up thy voice like a trumpet, and shew my people their

---

1. https://books2read.com/u/ba5XVy

2. https://books2read.com/u/ba5XVy

transgression, and the house of Jacob their sins." This verse is not merely a relic of ancient scripture but a timeless call that remains profoundly relevant today.

"Sounding The Call - The Voice of Conviction" is a deep exploration of Isaiah 58:1, its significance, and its pressing relevance for our contemporary world. This book looks into the heart of the prophet's mandate, examining the imperative to speak out against wrongdoing, to call out injustice, and to urge communities back to the path of righteousness. In an era where moral relativism often blurs the lines between right and wrong, the clarion call of Isaiah 58:1 reminds us of the unchanging standards of God's truth and the necessity of upholding them with courage and conviction.

Today, as in the days of Isaiah, the world is in desperate need of voices that are unafraid to speak the truth. The command to "cry aloud" is not just for the prophets of old; it is a charge to every believer to lift their voice against the injustices and sins that plague our societies. Whether it is addressing the deep-seated issues of inequality, corruption, or moral decay, the message of Isaiah 58:1 is a powerful reminder that silence is not an option when faced with evil. The call to "spare not" emphasizes the need for unwavering commitment to truth, even when it is inconvenient or unpopular. It challenges us to confront our own complacency and to take an active stand in the face of wrongdoing.

This book also explores the metaphor of the trumpet used in Isaiah 58:1—a symbol of urgency, clarity, and the need to capture attention. Just as a trumpet blast cuts through the noise, the voice of conviction must be bold and clear, leaving no room for ambiguity. In a time when many are reluctant to speak out for fear of criticism or backlash, "Sounding The Call" encourages readers to embrace their role as bearers of truth, to lift their voices without fear, and to stand firm in their convictions.

"Sounding The Call - The Voice of Conviction" is not just an exposition of Isaiah 58:1; it is a call to action. It invites readers to reflect on the relevance of this ancient text in their own lives and to consider how they can be voices of conviction in their communities. In exploring the need for prophetic voices today, this book challenges each of us to examine our own response to the injustices we see around us and to be willing to "cry aloud" in the pursuit of righteousness.

As you journey through these pages, may you be inspired to listen to the voice of conviction within you, to boldly proclaim the truth, and to live out the call of Isaiah 58:1 in a world that desperately needs it. The time to sound the call is now. The voice of conviction is yours to lift.

www.ingramcontent.com/pod-product-compliance
Lightning Source LLC
Chambersburg PA
CBHW051826130726
47987CB00003B/1429